E.K. Bond

DIA

ALSO BY MICHELE LEGGOTT

Like This? (Caxton, 1988)
Swimmers, Dancers (Auckland University Press, 1991)

DIA

Michele Leggott

AUCKLAND UNIVERSITY PRESS

Auckland University Press
University of Auckland
Private Bag 92019
Auckland

First published 1994

© Michele Leggott 1994

This book is copyright. Apart from fair dealing for the purpose of private study, research, criticism, or review, as permitted under the Copyright Act, no part may be reproduced by any process without the prior permission of Auckland University Press.

ISBN 1 86940 109 3

Publication is assisted by the Literature Programme of the Queen Elizabeth II Arts Council

Computerset in Berkeley
Printed by GP Print

Page layout of 'Where exactly are we?' by Lesley Kaiser and John Barnett; typesetting of 'Micromelismata' by Luke Williamson (Tradewinds Publishing, Devonport).

CONTENTS

'WHERE EXACTLY ARE WE?' 1

MICROMELISMATA 5

BLUE IRISES 9

    dia 10

    honeybee 17

    ladies mile 24

    seven from nine 31

    boat of heaven 38

CIRCLE 41

KEEPING WARM 55

ACKNOWLEDGEMENTS

Amending the Vulgar, ed. Mary Louise Browne and Ruth Watson (Wellington, 1992); Artspace, where 'Micromelismata' was part of *Word For Word 1991,* curated by Elizabeth Wilson; John Barnett/Lesley Kaiser, curators of *Like They Are Now* (November 1991) and *The Paper Project* (August 1992), where excerpts from some of these poems appeared; *Landfall; Otis Rush* (Adelaide); *Poetry New Zealand;* Radio New Zealand's Concert FM, with thanks to Elizabeth Alley for support and encouragement; *Sport;* Wellington City Art Gallery, which commissioned 'Where exactly are we?' as a ribbon text for *Now See Hear! : Art, language and translation* (July–September 1990), special thanks to Ian Wedde and exhibition designer Leon van den Eijkel; *West Coast Line* (Vancouver, Canada).

MATERIAL QUOTED

Fleur Adcock, from 'Ngauranga Gorge Hill,' *High Tide in the Garden* (1971).
Mary Barnard, from *Sappho: A New Translation* (1958).
Mary Ursula Bethell, *From a Garden in the Antipodes* (1929).
Eileen Duggan, from *New Zealand Bird Songs* (1929), *Poems* (1937), *New Zealand Poems* (1940), and *More Poems* (1951).
Bernadette Hall, from 'Constructing a Landscape,' *Heartwood* (1989).
Dinah Hawken, from 'Balance,' *It has no sound and is blue* (1987).
Robin Hyde, from *The Desolate Star* (1929), *The Conquerors* (1935), *Persephone in Winter* (1937), and *Houses by the Sea* (1952). Anne Ridler, from *The Nine Bright Shiners* (1943). Mary Stanley, from *Starveling Year* (1953, 1994).

Where are the women,

'WHERE EXACTLY ARE WE?'
Hawken "Balance"

↓

30's & 40's
geographical question.
2 islands not in our own seas' etc.
Location - marker of N.Z specialness.

Leggott rewriting and regendering nationalist
question. 'Where are we', 'the women' in all this?
Have to read in context with 'Opening the Archive'. Curnow's
altering of literary codes made it impossible to read Duggan + Hyde,
coming from diff. poetic.

INCANDESCENT LACUNAE FLUORESCE AT A

TOUCH **DESIRE** TORQUES DILOQUENT PEARL

CURVES LUMENS CON BRIO ALIGHT. NO BODY

EMBRACES ACHELESS **DESIRE** ELSE NOT

SENSE MY GARDENS LAMELLAE TO BEE

DESIDERATE MOUTH BRIGHT ALMOND

ABEILLE AMYGDALA AH OH ORIOLES

ROSEATE SANGLOTS LIKE LITT**ORAL** COMEDY

SWEET AND PELAGIC AMEN ONTO LOGICAL

2

DELIQUESCENCE OR LICKETY SPIT DELIGHT

FISHTAILS DEEP TROPES SQUIRT SQUID SUCK

OCTOPI PULL ANEMONES GULP AURELIA

GASPS   GOOSEBERRY   VISCERA   HOOT

COELENTERATE SOUP SIP SUP FOLLOW HER UP

SPIRULA SPIRULA THE HARD BIT IS GETTING

ASHORE WITH YOUR HYDROPHILE PURLING

DELIGHT INCUNABULA RAPT IN THE DARK

WITHOUT

MICROMELISMATA

an expressive vocal phrase or passage consisting of several notes sung to one syllable.

```
                    xxxxx      x     xxx
               xxx xxxxx   xxxx x  xx     xxx     x
                xxx   x xxxxxxxxxx xx xx     xxx xxxxx
               xxx xx xx xx xx  xx  xx xxx   xxx  xxxxx
              xxxxx x  x xx xx xx  xx x xxxxx  xxx          xx
                xx  xx xx xxxx xxx x  xx  xxxx   xxx  x  xxx
              xx xxxx x xx x xxxx xxx    xx x xxxxx  xxxxx x
             xx   xx x  x x xxxx xxxxx xx xx       x x  xxxx xxxxxx
            xxxxxx xxx xxxxxx xxxx xxxxxxxxxx   xx    xx          xxx
             xx xxx xxx xxx  xxxx xxxx  xxx  xxx    xxxx xxxxxxxx  x
            xx    x  xx     x  xxxxxx   x  x   x    xxxxx xxxxxxxxxx
           xx    xxxxxx xxxx     xxxxxx xx              xxxxxx  xxxxxxxx
           xx  xx xxxxxxxx       xx x                xx xxx         xxxx
          xxxx x xx xxxxx              x
         xxxxxxx    xxxxxxx
            xxxxxx
             xxxx
                                                                  xx
                                                              xxxxxxxx
             x                                          x x   xxx xxxxx
            xx         xx  x  x                        xx  xx xx x xxxxxx
           xxx xx xxxx x   xx                         xxx  xxx xx xxxx  xx
          xx xxx xxxx xx xxx x  xx   x              x  xxx  xx      xxxxxx
         xxxxxxxx x x xxxx x  xxx    xx x  x    xxx xxxxxxxx xxxxxx    x
         x xx xxxx xxxxx   xx xxx x xx x  xx   xx    xxxxx xx xxxxxx  x
         xxx xxx xxxxxx    x  xx x xx    x  xx xxx x  xx    xxxx    xx
          x xxx xxxxxx  xxxxx   x xx xxx   x xxx xxx xxx  x  x   xxx xx
           xxx   x  xxx xxxxxx xx xx x xxxxx  xx   x   xxxxx  xx
            xxx xxx xx   xxx xx xx xxxx xxx xx xxxxx    xxx xxxx
              x xxxx x xxx xxx xxxx xx xxx xx xxxxxxx xxxx
                xxxxxx xxx xxx xxxx xxx xx  xx   xxxx  xx
                  xx xxx  xx xx xx xxx xxx xxx xxxxxx
                   x  xxx x xx xxx  xx  xxxx  xx
                   xx xxx x xx xxx    xx xxxxx
                       xx xx x xxxx     x  xxxx
```

concrete poem

```
            micro      a   say
         coo melis kiss &  to     see    a
         coo & effortless to me   bee  white
         coo ee so be it in   oh yes  big noise
     print m & is in my  no  I print  you      we
         an em in your ear &  my kiss  can  I  say
         an iris & on I read raw  sh h sh know leave &
         em   on e  o & look shark  so &   oh  then daunce
         seeing her moment hear melodiously on  it         for
         to her you are such nice ass  for  isis desiring a
         to   & & do  a little   oh  s   o   gloss strawberry
         be melisma like   noises oh          loquat   orbiting
       so   no  sunlight      oh &          os etc       mist
    soft I am astir         &
 pressed redness
      before
      dark                                                              oh
                                                                     cherries
         I                                                       & I  her knave
       am   so  l o                     do  am of a valent
     not so very o  my                      you  all in time if
     to say able to tip I  ah  &          o say  my   little
     creamily o o toes & few   so   I  any euphoria female I
     & be muse naked so can I go  o  am   of sweet my fellow I
     for big mouths a do & on o  to  you & if  miel   do
     a fat mixing lucky & up oh  lip can or bit &  wag it
         paw & but damage is by a synch  be a  honey do
         paw lip do  all of my mama one it muses  due here
         a moue I saw her mime to din or kissing with
           tulips red pet pale hum in  do some us
           so now he is in and her big moment
             I was o we eat  as  rasp of
             am not I to her    an berry
             me li o toes   o read
```

BLUE IRISES

*Iris Wilkinson
(Robin Hyde)
Blue eyes.
'Reading by textual infra-red'
Leggott going blind.*

dia

I wanted to mouth you all over
spring clouds spring rain spring
tenderness of afternoons spent
blazing trails to this
place where breath roars through
the famous architecture of a poet's ear
Rose and peony buds and tongue
— ichthyous tumble honey and pearl —
the runner's foot has touched and adored
wistaria sprang after you, figs tipped
green air astounded by your passage
to the audient quays of the city
Now it begins, another voyage after nemesis
blue-eyed with the distance of it all

2

I didn't know about this passion

for oh she is also mine

delirium tympanis from the Portuguese

wind in her hair alongside us here

on the deck unhidden she slows your reading down

Fine ground darkness pours into the vessel

beans and flowers adorn the fall —

ichor! ichor! drink to the eyes locked on yours

the mouth that smiles and will speak for itself

I have always done the talking and she

put the words in my mouth saying do melisma

like sunlight be melisma like no sunlight pressed

redness before dark print an iris on her

& do melisma like sunlight astir oh & os etc

3

From the corner of this mouth take

kisses that begin in moonlight

and pitch slow fire over a history of you

reeling in the universe   Rhapsode

you and I have some walking to do, some

stitching together of the story so far, its feat

of silence, of sleeping lightly and listening

for the touch that outstrips all sense

in the hour before dawn   Look we have come

to the walled garden   See how the roses burn!

The lovers in the fountain spoon each other up

their drenched talk stretches the library resources

and when pubis and jawbone snick into place

you face my delight an uncontrollable smile

4

Honeyed learning!   I traced her once
to an island in spring, pointilliste mouse-ear
drifting down the margins   Then she was
phlyctena in the eye of the sea-ear reworking
a disturbance in my name   I found wild choral
allusions and scents that drew a white bee
to not-madness in the folds of her blue gown
This morning the whole world is wet wistaria
battered gutters running and everything drowning drunk
extends a big hand for the reprise
Which comes   Up the road on small trees
is a honey blue inflorescence I can't name
When the gardeners say cyanotis trust your ears
though rain fall into an open mouth

5

She made him a porpoise *gills a-snort*

because it was so hard to configure that body

The words weren't there or they rolled over

and supplied mermaids and mariners   For him

the language is a woman's body and she

will stand out in the rain a hundred years

running it back at him   Hast 'ou seen the rose

in the steeldust (or swansdown ever?)   Have

you seen a falcon stoop?   Hast thou found a nest

softer than cunnus?   Can yee see it brusle

like a Swan? O so white! O so soft! O so sweet

is she   The sonneteer coughs sneaks

another look at her dolphin scores out

the ellipse after *his vibrant tail*

6

within the temple gate and you knew

she was just delicious cooking up a storm

like this in the big kitchen of your heart

The bee in the fox-glove, the mouth on the nipple

Words! and be forgiven hot kisses translated

with cool accuracy She ripples past his *lilly*

in a Christal to get at a thyme-burning bee

shut up in a crystalline Perfect footwork

Bobble down that track loverboy they're bringing

out the focaccia bread studded with olives

and a rough red to match your breathing

She's a contrejour effect on the glittering sea

baby on the breast and a smile that makes your heart stop

Yes we bear sons They remember milk and honey

[handwritten: Fleur Adcock "Ngauranga Gorge Hill."]

7

Blue irises after dark

driving lamplight and Venice-glass

into a fine distraction : *bise* in a crystal line

wanting to know what you know and why

there's a smear of milk on my shirt so long

after weaning these heroes of eros

I planted incendiary kisses on solemn mouths

all over the island of matchless greed

whose trees see and know this and it grows

bees who mistake its name in a line of fire

run to delicate helices where they dance

orientation   Then what is before us

in the night wind where irises calibrate desire

and the rhyme is a voice like sunlight?

honeybee

Apex you'll come to one fine morning

set with that breakfast milk on the island steps

a full feast of fresh air under your belt

It's a small island, turtle in the channel

rare for the latitude, the islanders touchy

about a fragile domestic economy   Two

of them bang away at an extension to the house

dreamed up last night and being paid for

in green dollars   The Friday night pizzas

are legendary if you know which boat to get

and there on the rockface is the aretaloger's sign

sans me fatiguer ni de jour ni de nuit —

a little dairy factory by the name of Isis Lactans

pumping out soft cheeses of a truly divine nature

9

We could all go some more we could go down
for it ourselves and come back on the Cream Run
one quay at a time, mangos bagels wisdom
from the markets where you lean on one elbow
after making love and begin to make
the universe dooby doux to a tune that suits
your ripening sense of history
Going out for the makings, staying in to eat
mouth to mouth, why was it lost most
when we needed that contagion in the telling?
There is still the special place on her head
where they touch her for more of the story
while back in bed a sleep of hands and hearts
is airing nectar in all the generous mouths

10

How beautiful in jandals, o prince's daughter

the motive bones of your finely dusted feet

on the road to the cape and back

many summers past small clips of paradise

In the dark doorway the Fire Chief, a stir

of silver buttons and a ceremonial axe

as he walks into the picture again   His are the gifts

you are learning to take from the ballerina plate

piled high between you in all of his houses

Sometimes the regalia signifies, sometimes

it's just a couple of beers over lunch

watching your seventeen-year-old self descend

from the tree with the big nest of epiphytic lilies

to where he's waiting saying: Let's go, princess

11

To the north of Paradise a high summer moon

at four in the morning and I call out

the song of your body in the light of what is

before me   I know the precedents I'm looking for

the wise fire of intelligence in a body

that wants to metabolise lightning   I want

to get to the vineyard the river the mountain

the city and the sea undivided by your attentions

then I want to hammer out gamos everywhere

among the beautiful appetising trees of those places

So I get up in the dark and you call   Hey excelsa

your salty shoulder is first, sweet nicotiana next

but most from the open window to this wide bed

white scent from the tree of flowers   And sleep?

12

Schluck-schluck   perfect mind at work
on perfect body at the confluence of two rivers
called Melilot and Stamp   What a day
it's been salmon in the daypack at four thousand feet
high dives and honeypots into those piscine deeps
and a sweet precision of vocables throughout —
We've got it all as the islanders say, the ins and outs
the ups and downs, the map of the world
on the bedroom floor lost for so long, for so long
passed off as a hand to mouth myth among
painters who travelled the length of the country
to be close to its source   Look, the confluence
of two rivers, the deep relief of the map traversed
hop skip jump and free fall into the art of love

13

Apices that melt you femina climbing

the steps temple days and others minding

children or hanging out the sheets   How

transport is a word among vines —

excelsa and two young roe looking on

Carmel   Who would not forget her clear voice

remaking paradox as the shadow-hunt closes in

on the fabulous slopes of ellipsis:

And I light hearers to you   There she is

swallowed the sun and gives it back

each morning in the bright window *she's there*

on the tip of your tongue her bees working

the red flowers that take you from vine to fire

as she contemplates another shift in the pronouns:

14

I am the boat of heaven rocking outside

the orbit of the moon and the orbit of the sun

I am the dancer on the plate the one in blue

with a honey stomach full of delectable lies

I am the diver and the baker rolling over

and over in the dry grass which is most like rain

I am the parabola, a crural bow strung

across the single point of my dripping ascent

I am the eater of trees, the drinker of sense

and my name is the crown of a blue eye rising   Iris

I learned to write these languages   It is my kiss

on your mouth and there must be no fault

in the transmission   I am before you, I look

after you, I am a slow boat rocking everything

ladies mile

Silence has been important too, pharaoh
gliding through the lips of those who are asleep
Fig crop in my hands, lotus pool in flower
I was in another place when they came to me
and the bright edges of lacunae are seldom torn
by accident   Then fall off the edge of the earth
left hand under my head right embracing me
Why should you wish distance any greater than this?
I am quiet and we are writing in the throat
of all languages   The library at Alexandria burns
but my heart is a pool where the white birds step
among incipient papyri   A world of water
trims a world of fire for Osiris fluid in the blue
and gold of a moment's trust in the driving

16

Coming home like a derelict Egyptian, changing
worlds, a baby delivered in a jacaranda mist *just
like mine*   The trees are quiet now, the baby grown
and sorrow gone from the place it lay down in
long before I was born   What are we going to do
about that moon in the ngaio tree beating like
a fontanelle?   Can we go on reading the summer
constellations that do not pretend to be literature?
Cicadas   Avocados   But where's that frightening dog
sorrow?   *Lord butterfly on lord hibiscus spray*
are we through crying and the heart's big conversation
with pain?   Two sons, two sons and crowning
isn't a light word any more than a light kiss
resembles a dark one   Which you are

17

Suppose, sweet eyes, you went into a distant country

mad with the honey and the noon in your throat

a fiery drizzle of rip and glory asking: Where

are the words that broke the heart with beauty?

Not as plains that spread into us slowly, but as

a wind wet with carillons or winter's cold isthmus

in the azure year, you will find the frontiered heart

and write a script of stars across its salt and snow

Birds that think in oceans come and go, their chart

behind their eyes that scarcely sleep   Your mouth's adrift

with ghosts of fire the salt has burned to noontide

blue   Your sweetness ripples through the rain

of a country to which you may never return   You

are the still caesura that breaks a line in two

18

Leaf, leaf, how can I be sane enough

or mad enough to touch or leave untouched

what silence has to say?   Had I your eyes

your eyes I loved this lifetime, wonder's eyes

and the sun's voice against the nights of eaten moons

would my oppressions be healed?   Sometimes

fighting and dying are better than anything else

Back to the laughter of alien lips and eyes

how shall my heart find home?   I sleep

out of my bones so much bouquet just so much

bite in crystal those cool-dissolving wrists distil

from the sweet landfall water   It is dark

within daylight   The stranger is made of words

that swing by an island's shadow

19

Smile at that mountain where love was

eaten on a morning when the world held still

in the rain's embrace a promise of iris blue

In the heart every moment a splitting of the moon

in the belly picnics of sky and dancing zephyrs

Be loved be happy, feed and be fattened on this —

A weekend in winter lemon butter thickening

over slow heat, two candy boys ecstatic

on the juicer, Persian mystics on top of the fridge

glinting elevation and excess   Stir and shout

give them *(feet off the green couch right now)* the works!

The parrots of my soul have begun to chew sugar

they turn up the deck and dance loopsville

one in my arms whirled in a golden mirror

20

Running water you are the phoenician's mouth
lute-curved and eating his dreams like flame
I have lost the light of your laughter very cool
and sweet the breath of limes or an aureole
of waters falling where a hand might cup the breast
of one who like the young moon is white
and strange and slender   The gleaming human
lamp on your mad ship's shoulder is a woman
drawn up by the fine chain of silence white
and unbroken about her neck   Her full breast
pours out a mirth of stars, bright areolae
or glittering revolution in heaven's cool
breathing of lines which set the double-curved flame
of the lover sea against her laughing mouth

21

Jewelling, or if the Silenced laugh

memory from the wheel of white stars turning

against the sky, what should the thought of my heart

do but flood out the empty heavens?   These were

my children, my beloved   Take them, hold them forever

as you held them first, small bodies motive

in a sea of air and learning the warm animal

from us all walking in the houses of the sun

Lifts, utter mirror of his hand on the wheel

the strategy of repeats that still gesture him

live in a world filling with the tears of Isis

We have been sad too long   Close up this desolate

house and drive to where the island's wet light

candours the moon on the river wider than a smile

seven from nine

he made her a dolphin *luce di femina*

sent her the dream of himself a sailboat

in costume and she read all night luculent

sheets and the arrowy glimpsing curve

he made between them   she is the lucida

planing ahead of the moments utterance owes

a stir of roses at the edge of space *lumina*

fragrans light as air that is anadyomene

in his bursting lungs   double and lucent

her purposes jump the white boat of the sky

fine fins under the keel for the pellucid

Sisters   *the stars are not in her counting*

and stole the line of dancers enlumined there

in a pageant of mirrors   nine bright shiners

23

leaving history and its folios leafing over

an alphabet of twigs *until the stript sentences move*

as a woman's limbs under cloth   o dearest floss

those trees against the blue gown of evening how

I need their writing on the backs of my eyes and you

a light breeze among words with lamellate fingers

it's so simple   a destination and a curse reading

or talking love's ascendant in times of perfidy

I wept at the cutting down *for no other tree like it*

grows out of the earth drops honey and turns the world

on its head   zu-bird I will leave you out

of this wood I stepped into when I misted their eyes

and vanished   my spick buds corroborate the joke

we are leaving history into leaving history

24

walk out to the legend's rim the row

of footlights crosswise of the roll *moisopolon*

domos but truly it is a house of dance we trace

from torn scripts and drawings chalked on a board

there is a great deal more of it rehearsed

in empty rooms where fates are made up as we go

over the ground in carriages of air and sinew

waiting with the others for a jubilation

thiasos my pearly necklace, confidantes and

analeptic friends, here is the recension

after stage death and a kind of adornment

stripped in for going lengthwise of the poem

Mouth   carry me to the last word which is not

Jewel   if ever you would for the world where

25

do you remember how a golden broom
grows on the sea beaches?   who will love you
shoulders carved in bone and mother of pearl
a set of collarbones shaped *with a love true*
like papaya on the inside, lenticular
and potable as slow kisses *when your rambling*
in the bladed certainties of the craft
skiffs to the point where whole *days are gone*
before breakfast is cleared or the sand swept
from everybody's sheets   the bach became
a house to live in all year round the kids
were born with a fresh colloquial directness
and sapphics stuck like magic to their tongues
in what appears to be a deliberate use

26

of ambiguity   but we were dark

and drove both ways because sounds of grief

are unbecoming in a poet's household

and not suitable in ours   strawberries grow

in the sea the northern claw gathers light

noises from the mouth of Zubenelgenubi

counting brilliants for the lamp that swings

between us on the mountain of the meridian

still there is the dark crossing a lullaby spun

perilune for measure over the smooth muscle

of the diastole : a crib a coffin a boat

a fish in the wood the embrace of cold knowledge

by warm balance beating out paradigmatic

rhythms on the lettery door of the fridge

27

what my heart meant in the next apartment

zooming colures overhead like a white net

dropped over the bed   and we chanteused romance

at the Agapanthus Motel till its sides split

and the room was full of laughter   the awful pun

of abundance frolicking bare naked up the hall

a rumpled irony of linen metonymically

discarded by the fiducial angels of the house —

beatitudinal bloom!   be violet tiaras in tune

with celestial mechanics   o memes tinkling

in the afternoon *you're so graced*

to be placed pink-ankled in orbit at

the imagined corners with all these bodies

making a song and dance about conjunction

28

Make me a heaven in a huluppu bed, noon

on the wing and the little seahorse in the brain

richly doped with pleasures that transform

their provenance   it's my boat

she touched many places but still it was here

air rose and the hot flowery cliffs entranced

you who circle that threshold where grief dies

fooling the limits of a wild civility, we

breathed as one the other childhood's ache

for an utmost to reify the heartbeats

of hyperbole   *Phainetai moi*

yes *without equal* fat tamure snapping up

the estuary or melting in the mouth, I wait

for you just two steps short of the measure

boat of heaven

Dark sweet city deal me your optic

due east of the superluminal and beyond

the unavoidable nerve jewelled and naked

which prints the flaming wings of a chord

ondoyant across the whistle bones

we play at tumult's feast   in old houses

colonnaded by the full melisma

nine times the singular fault repaired *she is me*

the sister you buried as a vanished alpha

tore the figured ground apart   tell us

how you survived those retinal meanders

on the mind's dark floor   for what keeps you

irrefrangible in the bright sun's arc

trades my sadness to a wealth of stars

30

blue iris in the winds of March darken

that heart my dancer whose avowals are

in broad sunlight as the fountain's spray

on bare shoulders patterned by the shadow

of a dream   how real and how easy this scene

by the sea pink as coral the beautiful voice

of a liar wheeling in space *sky's violin*

sure of nothing but the vision in the window

passing flawless to its next appointment

telluric roses of Pieria and the deified throne

traced where a white himation dropped softly

from revelation's shoulder makes joy

light as a component of the universe

outside the exit points to time

CIRC(L)E

*

  the heart in its cage stands up
  desiring fine instruments
      what
      shall we play?

  laughter startles the sublime lyric
  c'est le pays du désir   Bethell (Primavera)
      and I
      its best
      gesture
 wake in tears

 the heart in its cage stands up
 desiring fine instruments what shall we play?
 laughter startles the sublime lyric *c'est*
 le pays du désir and I its best gesture
 wake in tears

*

who sees me in a winter house bare-soled
on the warm slate or looking into the flames
of a September fire?   the room is filled
with shadows *rich beyond desire* I sit
listening to the beat of the sea and the wind
in the courtyard trees   the xenia waits
yes always   and looks most perfectly
like itself   I raise the hand that opens
eyes of black glass and soundless anchorage
then sends the absent deer into the hunter's path —
eat and sleep beside your beach fires and the boat
pulled up under the cliff   the rest is easy

visions come

there on the breast of Ocean little fascicle
bound for the black island of sunrise
vitreous distances announce you to the citadel
clear across the stations of the amber route
there she has her home and her dancing-lawns
lift and fall small shadow on the breast
without substance or moment you strike
the shape of a sail against my living skin

I breathe it closer

the drugs will fail once
for deeper than narcosis runs the enchantment
alphabets and strings would save you from
his pharmakon I grew his trickery I turn
to my account   there can be no weapons between us
but numbers falling in a dark place
and the click of sea-glass beads

then I will know who you are

a goddess or a woman they said
and took no chances   for this civility
the house ate them and because they were not you
walking up to the polished doors halting
my work for the ritual of stranger into house guest
made captive by the whiff of beauty and design
wind harps shaping the island's name
dumb silvery eyes warping along at my hem
catspaw on the meniscus   an exophoria of sea wolves
and yourself   when that ridiculous herb fell
from your belt I laughed

to myself

moon humour at midday now you have reached the end
of the colonnade with its view of blue waters
risen over white silica *that entranced touch* irises
pushed aside the house laid open to swiftness
high above the literal

contingency

* *

I want to transpose this moon
make two in the moon make room for two
in the space of a single   O   sibilant
lunations talking in the leaves together
hiss of prophecy   this we did and stood apart
and let black terror spin the oracles awry
otherwise ruin otherwise nothing
in the world beyond the iris gates

closer my face to the winter sea
white under weightless dancing after
nineteen years drawing water in a wide harbour
ardour shakes the vine the walls fall down around me
yes always   and on comes the blue moon whistling
about luck or startling accidents of history
swim, moon—   this is the harbour I love you from
these my doubled songs pulling you round again

* *

let there be couscous a lark and a dove
who flies out above the white shingle paths
then pours herself back into the trees
her house is a selection from the first fifteen hundred
odes and lyrics and all of them praise the sight
of you naked and asleep on the bed beside me
silver light shimmies over the dark bowl of the ceiling
cool afternoon allegory as elegant
as the alighting dove and her citric rustle in the grandiflora tree
dark ground dark room shadows
to catch what is carried by the light and to convulse
under its impact   chaos to chiasma and back

a precise imaging of desire

the fish-infested seas have yielded you
my foot in silhouette against the open doorway
toe to the cushion star above
other stencillings disposed across the evening sky
when your ship is on a star its beautiful markings
render any text corrupt that cannot sing
a very young remote and slender but outshining
but all predominant moon

make your wish

initiate and aware in latticed orchards
around the full house of Ocean's black daughter
appetite sparkles about the day the night the new year
any time of year but most particularly now
decked out in black-heart cherries
exuberant richness feeds you darkness sustains
the circles of your outward sailing world
so richly at odds with this dark fame

and what have you

the pigs are apocryphal someone else's
fabulation signing off the curve of the joke
we lived *sine pigmento*   there were feasts and entertainments
fireworks music over water and the care of children
how they fought and swam and slept out   whole nests
of straight limbs and eyelid waves   whole picnics
to be transcribed into the night sky
where no one forced the exaltation of larks
because they seemed to take care of themselves
moonlight silvers all these fruit tree tops
birds waves words I have said it before

yes always

in circadian measures
with an eye on the moon in its net of branches
and looking on the dazzled cones
of the island

* * *

Also there is an unpublished one
they pass Remembered peach-tree islands
where over a shingled cobhouse came
Shadows of things far lovelier than their shapes
the green parrakeets, and shared the
Wild fuchsias' falling crimson dyes the sands
'Plenty for all to eat' in Miss Beth
where one house Sets drift-fires to the night
ell's peach-orchard of early days.   This
Past stars grown big as fists, through dangerous reefways
poem needs some rearrangement but
there's a cool web of language winds us in
shouldn't be left out of any New
Hyades Pleiades Symplegades all
Zealand anthology.   I know those old,
Shadows of things are lovelier than their shapes
scarcely obtainable, honey-peaches
Ambergris rolls on Hellfire Beach

* * *

when you go I will send you
through the old rivers of lamentation and pain
with better charts than the story provides
in the small hours of its twenty four books
what do they know
of a night wind on the hillside where not the poet but
my hand plays ghost above the flattened wake
of a black ship sailing into hell   gold and silver
I passed you at the outset and unforgetting lapis
stolen out of your wind shadow to take
line honours   yes I will be there
but not as you see me now

scotoma sings

to a child jumping in spray above the bouncing mat
that presses cool water through an open weave
he's trying to fly, remembering
the nets of perception *upheaved among remembrance*
soft patter of water recurrent thud of body
body's recurrent thud and water pattering
soft genitives and bright participles in the summer garden
sailor of the new wine the years of making you fly
rapt in the dark without

fear now

the descent un-
fathomed running unbound to unreadable
ends filaments cut kevlar ripped apart
with a sound of thunder come to grief
on august Persephone's wall   you are dead meat
stripped and beaten
the cord most perfectly strung that hangs you there
with nothing but the outline of your restless double
to beg the question of this quiet excarnation
in the palace of disasters

is she weeping

reefs
propounding a phosphorescent scar
become the cursor trimmed with silver tears
scanning vengeance in a circle   dead volcanic tips
disturb the surface of an ocean's rolling eye
and through that sparkling rip the dark will ride
even to the city of visible acumen   *best jester*
the hard bit is getting ashore with nothing
to go on but a few bloody fragments
and the faint praise of insects

in extremis

as you walk towards another wisp of smoke
rising above the trees   *when I close my eyes*
you are there when I open them you are marvelling
at the woman in the firelight who has stopped singing

to smile at your approach

* * * *

Eight Belles steaming up the harbour
and one between the heads
watching love go

to an island with a library
a sign at the gate
saying
      BLOW
      HORN
           in the long allee

where the golden queens
their red hearts wine grapes and peacocks
hunt the wild harbour home

* * * *

KEEPING WARM

you there at
the long end
of my arm

drive me to
work & back
over the bridge

to distraction
icecreams in
the wind or

moon on the
beach : *them
dauphins*

berserk about
us on their
offshore roads

razzle dazzle
moonlight
climb up the

near side of
heaven's cloudy
smile : this is

heaven & you
in it following
la vie dansante

warm rowdy
voice reading
to the kids

draped word
perfect about
you doing

equal parts
charm & need
for me looking

on decoding
nuance (oh
clouds) the house

needs a paint
the Saturday
skilsaws howl

into September
& cups of tea
punctuate the

hard questions
: there was a
moment when

that look in
your eye closed
all distances

ka-boom as
the poets say
dreamily

two people
get together
like *spring*

and *moon*
time & place
fold around

them : yes
there's specific
moonlight and

a curve in
the road where
it takes your

breath away
this is local
right here up

close & it's
your bridge to
where I stand

laughing at
it already
written in

big glittering
letters : let's
go out there

and do the poem

note
We can all write heart poems, the ones that take breath away or make tears and laughter come. Or they release the little zing that is desire. You want to write bits down, hear it again, play it again (that's hunger). You keep them by you, within reach (sufficiency). Sometimes they ride around with you for days at a time. Sometimes they step from the shadows when you were thinking about something else entirely. You ignore the tearing sound at your peril; they always have something to say. We work in the dark, they say, we do what we can. We give what we have. Our doubt is our passion. Our passion is our task. The rest is the madness of art. You can quote me.

   Have you seen, they ask, the rose in the steel dust? or swansdown ever? Have you heard sweetness ripple through the rain? Femina, femina, that would not be dragged into paradise: how can I be sane enough or mad enough to touch or leave untouched what silence has to say? The olfactory floor's a-hum. O taste and see; chew, swallow, and transform.

   Vocatives, interrogatives, imperatives. If I thought I was on my own I would give it away. I work with the others, listening and talking back, picking up the conversations over distance, following instructions or making them up. What I am looking for is the perfect poem, what I am doing in the interim is paying out attention and reeling in language.

   I want heart but I want scope too. Big projects for poetry, like raiding and rewriting its androcentric history. I am not interested in the one-page poem unless it is a constituent of something bigger, unless its brevity is a training ground so I can read to marathon length. This is where complexity comes in, and I welcome it. Complexity is about endurance, about surviving over time and distance to ask old questions in new places.

What I have written mixes up these things because it is both lyrical and investigative. Some of the time it investigates lyricism, using lyric poetry to find out who writes it, and why, and why that should be so. 'Blue Irises' in particular tries to catch this doubleness of looking. It has a big cast, so many voices having their say, but ultimately the cast-list is just seven: I, you, he, she, we, you (all), and they. Moving the seven around history makes the voices speak again in new contexts, and often they are extremely beautiful, or moving, or both. I wanted them for that and because I needed their aggregate to write, or rewrite, some of the oldest stories we tell each other. There is no way of telling where one bit-part finishes and another starts; and it is only my voice signing to the first person pronouns.

Some of the poems here stare down the literary oblivion of several New Zealand women poets, looking for what was lost when we asserted that good poetry in this country was shaped exclusively by British-derived Modernism of the 1930s and 1940s. It is time we listened in other places in order to draw some of those shadowy figures back into the conversation about language and place. To this end I have practised a kind of ventriloquism, picking out white-hot lines from the poems of (among others) Robin Hyde and Eileen Duggan and recombining them with an ear for the heart, complexity, and engagement with which they were written. This is homage.

It has also shown me how to make a matrix where none was visible or audible. It is a kind of speaking together, problematic but full of possibilities. When I was then able to connect the language and preoccupations of these poets with a largely disappeared tradition of singing women that took me sometimes off the maps of literacy itself, I began to understand why their writing exerted such a hold once I knew how to listen.

M.L.